Bruno Mars

By Adrianna Morganelli

Crabtree Publishing Company
www.crabtreebooks.com

Crabtree Publishing Company

www.crabtreebooks.com

Author: Adrianna Morganelli
Publishing plan research and development:
  Reagan Miller
Editorial director: Kathy Middleton
Editors: Molly Aloian, Crystal Sikkens
Proofreader and Indexer: Wendy Scavuzzo
Photo research: Crystal Sikkens
Designer: Ken Wright
**Production coordinator and prepress
  technician:** Ken Wright
Print coordinator: Margaret Amy Salter

Photographs:
Associated Press: page 22
© Fox/Courtesy: Everett Collection: page 24
Getty Images: Focus on Sport: page 6; Kevin
  Mazur/WireImage: page 8; Gavin Roberts/
  Rhythm Magazine: page 10; Dave J Hogan:
  page 16; Dan MacMedan/WireImage: page 17;
  Ethan Miller: page 18; Nick Pickles/
  WireImage: page 21; Jeff Vespa/WireImage:
  page 27
Keystone Press: wenn.com: pages 11, 26;
  FAME Pictures: cover, page 19; Media
  Punch/Unimedia: page 28
Keysonte Press Canada: Media Punch: page 25
Photofest: Columbia Pictures: page 9;
  NBC: page 20
Anka Agency/Photoshot: pages 12, 13
Shutterstock: s_bukley: pages 1, 15; Joe Seer:
  page 5; DFree: page 7; Featureflash: page 14;
  Helga Esteb: page 23
massimo barbaglia/Marka/SuperStock: page 4

Library and Archives Canada Cataloguing in Publication

Morganelli, Adrianna, 1979-, author
      Bruno Mars / Adrianna Morganelli.

(Superstars!)
Includes index.
Issued in print electronic formats.
ISBN 978-0-7787-0020-3 (bound).--ISBN 978-0-7787-0041-8
(pbk.).--ISBN 978-1-4271-9382-7 (pdf).--ISBN 978-1-4271-9376-6
(html)

      1. Mars, Bruno, 1985- --Juvenile literature. 2. Musicians--
United States--Biography--Juvenile literature. I. Title.
II. Series: Superstars! (St. Catharines, Ont.)

ML3930.M363M84 2013   j782.42164092   C2013-905227-5
                                            C2013-905228-3

Library of Congress Cataloging-in-Publication Data

Morganelli, Adrianna, 1979-
      Bruno Mars / Adrianna Morganelli.
          pages cm. -- (Superstars!)
      Includes index.
      ISBN 978-0-7787-0020-3 (reinforced library binding : alk.
  paper) -- ISBN 978-0-7787-0041-8 (pbk. : alk. paper) -- ISBN
  978-1-4271-9382-7 (electronic pdf : alk. paper) -- ISBN 978-1-
  4271-9376-6 (electronic html : alk. paper)
      1. Mars, Bruno, 1985---Juvenile literature. 2. Musicians--
United States--Biography--Juvenile literature. I. Title.

ML3930.M318M67 2013
782.42164092--dc23
[B]
                                                    2013036658

Crabtree Publishing Company
www.crabtreebooks.com   1-800-387-7650

Printed in Canada/102013/BF20130920

Published in Canada
Crabtree Publishing
616 Welland Ave.
St. Catharines, ON
L2M 5V6

Published in the United States
Crabtree Publishing
PMB 59051
350 Fifth Avenue, 59th Floor
New York, New York 10118

Published in the United Kingdom
Crabtree Publishing
Maritime House
Basin Road North, Hove
BN41 1WR

Published in Australia
Crabtree Publishing
3 Charles Street
Coburg North
VIC 3058

CONTENTS

Words that are defined in the glossary are in
bold type the first time they appear in the text.

Out of This World

A man of many talents, Bruno Mars is a singer, songwriter, and record **producer**. He has been called one of the best songwriters of his generation, and his smooth high voice has attracted a legion of fans. Bruno has sold more than 8 million albums worldwide as a singer, and more than 100 million albums writing and producing for other artists.

Bruno learned to play the guitar because he was a big fan of Jimi Hendrix.

A Man of Many Talents

One of the most **versatile** singers in pop music, Bruno's music is a combination of rock, reggae, R&B (rhythm and blues), soul, and hip hop. He has released two wildly successful albums, which have topped the charts all over the world. His hit singles "Locked Out Of Heaven," "Grenade," "Just the Way You Are," and "When I Was Your Man," can be heard on radio stations everywhere. Bruno has been a performer all his life. His live shows are full of energy, and fans can't help but sing and dance along when he is on stage. Bruno's talent hasn't gone unnoticed. He has been nominated for many awards, going on to win one Grammy, one American Music Award, one Billboard Music Award, and a BRIT Award.

Bruno won the award for Favorite Pop/Rock Male Artist at the 2011 American Music Awards.

Stage Name

Bruno Mars uses a stage name; his real name is Peter Gene Hernandez. The name Bruno is a nickname that his father gave him when he was two years old, because he reminded him of the legendary wrestler Bruno Sammartino. Bruno found that his last name, which is Puerto Rican, caused music labels to **stereotype** him. Many people assumed he was a Latin singer. He adopted the last name Mars because he says he felt like he didn't have any pizzazz. Also, he jokes, girls have told him that he is out of this world, so he figured it was like he was from Mars!

Bruno Sammartino was one of the most popular American wrestlers of the 1960s and early 1970s. He was one of the longest-running wrestling champions.

He Said It

"My dad was a fan of the wrestler Bruno Sammartino, who was heavyset. When I was a kid I was a little pudgy. I reminded him of a wrestler."
—Commenting on his nickname in an interview in *NY Daily News*, 2010.

Fedora

Who would have thought that a simple hat had the power to help launch a music career? Bruno Mars is rarely seen not wearing his **signature** fedora. About six months before his music career took off, Bruno won $600 playing poker in a casino in Los Angeles. He had just cut his hair and felt strange with less hair on his head. He stopped into a menswear store in the casino and bought the gray fedora that now defines his look. Having worn it during many performances, interviews, and music videos, the hat soon began to fall apart. He left the original fedora at his mother's home in Hawaii for safekeeping.

Bruno has since purchased countless fedoras in different styles and colors.

A Star Is Born

On October 8, 1985, Peter Gene Hernandez was born in Honolulu, Hawaii. He and his brother and four sisters were raised in the neighborhood of Waikiki. Growing up in tropical Waikiki, where reggae is very popular, helped shape the way Bruno would later write and perform his music.

Musical Family

Bruno Mars was born into a musical family. His father Peter is a **percussionist** from Brooklyn, New York. His mother Bernadette was a singer and dancer who **immigrated** to Hawaii from the Philippines as a child. His parents met in Hawaii while performing in a show in which Peter played percussion and Bernadette was a hula dancer.

Bruno's father and his band played as the opening act at one of Bruno's concerts in Hawaii.

Little Elvis

As Bruno grew up, music and performing became a part of his everyday life. His uncle was an Elvis Presley impersonator who encouraged Bruno to learn Elvis's lyrics and dance moves. By the age of four, Bruno was impersonating Elvis in his family's band called The Love Notes. He also performed songs by Michael Jackson, the Isley Brothers, and The Temptations. Word of the tiny performer quickly spread across the island, and Bruno became a local celebrity.

VIVA LAS VEGAS

When Bruno was five years old, he was featured in a Hawaiian magazine called *Midweek*. The feature caught the attention of movie executives and, in 1992, Bruno earned a **cameo** in the movie *Honeymoon in Vegas*, starring Nicolas Cage.

A scene from *Honeymoon in Vegas* shows Bruno is a natural at impersonating Elvis!

School Days

During the day, Bruno attended elementary school with his friends, but five nights a week, he pulled on his sequined jumpsuit to perform with his family. School soon became less important to him. Instead of paying attention to his lessons, Bruno thought about the fun he would have performing that night. As he got older, he also started impersonating Michael Jackson. Imitating these famous stars gave Bruno the chance to learn about performing and singing in front of audiences.

A Variety of Music

Bruno's family exposed him to many different types of music as a child, including rock, hip hop, R&B, and reggae. In Hawaii, reggae is played on every major radio station, and the local bands have adopted the sound of reggae from Jamaican legend Bob Marley. Bruno feels that reggae is popular in Hawaii because the music brings people together.

Everyone in Bruno Mars's family sings or plays an instrument. His older brother Eric is a great drummer and left the police force to be in Bruno's band!

Musical Influences

During high school, Bruno listened to American R&B artists such as Jodeci and Keith Sweat, 1950s rock, Motown, and classic rock bands including Led Zeppelin, The Police, and the Beatles. He was also influenced by doo-wop, which is a style of rhythm-and-blues music that highlights vocals instead of instruments. Bruno's love of music inspired him to learn to play several instruments, including bass, piano, congas, and guitar.

THE LYLAS

Bruno's four sisters, Presley, Jaime, Tahiti, and Tiara, formed a music group called The Lylas, which stands for "love you like a sister." They haven't released an album yet, but have a recording deal.

The Lylas also have plans to star in a new reality series that will follow them as they leave their life in Hawaii and move to Los Angeles to record their debut album.

The School Boys

While attending President Theodore Roosevelt High School in Honolulu, Bruno and his friends formed a band called The School Boys. They performed songs from classic oldies bands including The Isley Brothers and The Temptations. The School Boys performed alongside Bruno's family's band The Love Notes at the Ilikai Hotel in Honolulu. Bruno credits his childhood performances for the comfort that he feels while on stage today.

American Idol

Peter Hernandez

In high school, Bruno was voted "American Idol" by his classmates.

Taking a Chance

Bruno was determined to make it big in the music industry. After graduating from high school in 2002, he moved to Los Angeles, California, to do just that. Bruno has said that moving to Los Angeles was a culture shock for him. He found that life was more fast-paced there than it was in Hawaii. The following year, he was signed with Motown Records. But landing a record deal was not all that he had dreamed. Although Bruno could sing and perform, he was inexperienced as a recording artist, and he was dropped by the label. He soon

Bruno was only 17 years old when he graduated from high school and ventured to Los Angeles to pursue his dream.

became **disillusioned** with the music industry. But little did he know that his initial failure would lead to a new venture—one that would eventually propel him into stardom.

He Said It

"I might have cried. I might have shed some tears. You definitely have those nights where you feel a little insecure, but I didn't want to give up. My goal was, 'I'm not going to go back home. I'm not going back to Hawaii and face my friends and my family saying it didn't pan out. I've got to do something.'"
—In an interview with Piers Morgan, about being dropped by Motown Records, 2012

Another Chance

Bruno's time with Motown Records led him to meet songwriter and producer Philip Lawrence, who was also signed to the label. They began writing songs together and later joined with another friend, **engineer** Ari Levine. The three formed the production team The Smeezingtons. In 2006, Lawrence introduced Bruno to Aaron Bay-Schuck, the **artists and repertoire (A&R)** manager at Atlantis Records. Bruno played guitar and sang some of his songs for him. Bay-Schuck loved Bruno right away, but the label's other executives weren't as excited. Instead, Bay-Schuck hired The Smeezingtons to write and produce songs for other artists signed to Atlantis.

GRAMMY AWARDS

Bruno and The Smeezingtons attended the 54th annual Grammy Awards. Bruno was nominated for six awards, but unfortunately did not win.

Song Producers

The Smeezingtons produced songs for many artists including Alexandra Burke, Adam Levine, Sean Kingston, Brandy, K'naan, and Flo Rida, among others. In 2009, The Smeezingtons underwent a week-long series of writing sessions at Atlantis with artists B.o.B, Travie McCoy, and Lupe Fiasco. It was this work—B.o.B.'s song, "Nothin' On You," and Travie McCoy's "Billionaire"—that helped skyrocket Bruno's reputation within the music industry. Both songs became worldwide hits, and Bruno sang on both tracks. His high voice was instantly recognizable, and he also starred in the music videos, smiling beneath his signature gray fedora. His work on the tracks strengthened his relationship with Atlantis, and he was signed with the label as an artist that year.

WAVIN' FLAG

Bruno helped write the song "Wavin' Flag" by K'naan. The song became the theme song for the 2010 Vancouver Winter Olympics.

Lupe Fiasco also sang a version of the song "Nothin' On You," but Atlantic Records gave B.o.B. the song instead.

15

Blasting Onto the Scene

While The Smeezingtons worked with other artists, they were also frantically writing songs for Bruno's first album *Doo-Wops & Hooligans*. Although primarily a pop album, many songs on *Doo-Wops & Hooligans* have elements of rock, reggae, R&B, hip hop, and soul music. *Doo-Wops & Hooligans* produced many hit singles, including "Just the Way You Are," "Marry You," "Grenade," and "The Lazy Song."

Bruno Mars holds the cover of his debut album (left) with his fellow songwriters from The Smeezingtons.

He Said It

"It explains the two sides of me. Doo-wop is a special form of music I grew up on. It's straight to the point, very simple. I have songs like that ... I have that simple, romantic side of me but I'm also just a young, regular dude and that's like the hooligan side!"
—On the title of his album in an interview with 4Music, 2010

"Just the Way You Are"

Before Bruno's debut album was released, many singles were played on the radio to **promote** the album. His lead single "Just the Way You Are" was released on July 20, 2010. It is a feel-good song with a beat that listeners can't help dancing to, and a chorus that is easy to sing along with. In it, a man is telling a woman that she doesn't need to fuss with her hair and makeup because she looks beautiful just as she is. The love song became one of the best-selling singles of all time.

GRAMMY WINNER

On February 13, 2011, "Just the Way You Are" won the Grammy Award for Best Male Pop Vocal Performance.

Winning Best Male Pop Vocal Performance gave Bruno his first Grammy Award!

The Downside to Fame

Bruno quickly discovered that being a star brought many perks, including adoring fans, money, and special treatment at restaurants and clubs. But just as quickly, he experienced the downside of being a celebrity. Just as "Just the Way You Are" rose to number one, Bruno was arrested in the bathroom of the Hard Rock Casino in Las Vegas for possession of drugs. He was ordered to pay a $2000 fine, perform 200 hours of community service, and complete a drug counseling course. After fulfilling the requirements, the charges were then erased from his criminal record.

After his arrest for drug possession, Bruno learned an important lesson: that all of the rewards of his success could easily be taken away.

He Said It

"You've prepped your whole life. It's all you know how to do. You're a kid experiencing life in…Sin City, and that was the lesson: It can all be taken away. Put you in a weird place. Embarrass you."
——in *GQ* magazine, April 2013

"Grenade"

Bruno's second single "Grenade" was released in September 2010. It is one of the few songs on the album with a dark theme. It is a song about the emotional and physical struggle to convince a girl of his devotion. In the music video, Bruno is dragging a piano through the streets of Los Angeles to sing to the woman he loves, only to find her with another man. "Grenade" reached number one on the Billboard Hot 100. Everything Bruno touched seemed to turned to gold. His full debut album had not yet been released and already he was being catapulted to stardom!

The music video for "Grenade" earned three nominations at the 2011 MTV Video Music Awards.

Doo-Wops & Hooligans

Bruno's debut album made a big impression on the music world. Most of the songs are optimistic and have a carefree vibe to them, and are about love, friendship, and fun. Music critics praised his smooth voice because it easily fits a range of musical styles. The album was released on October 4, 2010, rocketing Bruno to the top of the charts. The album, which sold more than six million copies worldwide, forced the world to take him seriously as an artist.

Bruno promoted his new album by performing "Just the Way You Are," "Nothin' on You," and "Grenade" as the musical guest on *Saturday Night Live* on October 9, 2010.

Touring

Two days after *Doo-Wops & Hooligans* was released, Bruno hit the road to open for the band Maroon 5 during their Hands All Over Tour. He then toured with Travie McCoy throughout Europe at sold-out venues in Scotland, Germany, England, France, and Sweden. The Bruno Mars Live: Doo-Wops & Hooligans Tour began on November 16, 2010. The first **leg** of the tour was performed in the United States and it ended with two shows in his native state of Hawaii in December. Bruno then toured throughout Europe, Asia, the Caribbean, and South America, performing a total of 103 shows.

Going Home

While Bruno was in Los Angeles trying to break into the music business, he promised himself that he would never return to

The first stop on the second leg of the Doo-Wops & Hooligans Tour was in London, England, on January 24, 2011.

Hawaii as a failure. During his Doo-Wops & Hooligans Tour, he returned home as anything but! Millions of fans awaited his homecoming concert, including his family, who were proud of the name that Bruno made for himself.

Unorthodox Music

Bruno Mars wanted his second album to be like his stage shows: rowdy and energetic. The album is called *Unorthodox Jukebox*, and represents Bruno's freedom to write and record whatever he wanted. Bruno says that the album turned into something soulful, electronic, and experimental. It sounds like the album title was a perfect fit!

SESAME STREET STAR

In 2011, Bruno was a guest star on the children's television program *Sesame Street*. He sang a song called "Don't Give Up" with the Muppets, who provided the background vocals.

"Locked Out Of Heaven"

Bruno's lead single off of *Unorthodox Jukebox*, entitled "Locked Out Of Heaven," was an instant success, topping the Billboard Hot 100 chart in the United States for six weeks straight. It also reached the top ten on the charts of more than 20 countries around the world. Many critics noted that the song's style and sound is similar to tracks by the British rock band The Police. Although Bruno has always been influenced by The Police, he insists that the similarities were not intentional.

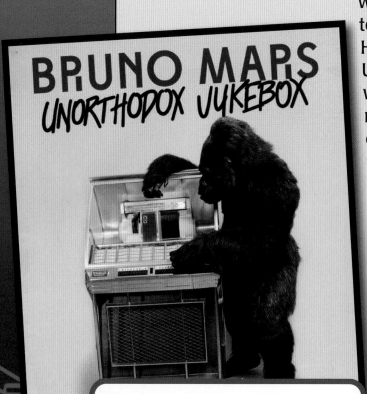

BRUNO MARS
UNORTHODOX JUKEBOX

Unorthodox Jukebox is a pop and R&B album, but other musical **genres** are included as well, such as soul, rock, and reggae.

"When I Was Your Man"

"When I Was Your Man" is the second single on *Unorthodox Jukebox*. It is a **ballad** about heartbreak, and only Bruno's voice and the piano can be heard on the track. In it, he sings about the regret he feels at letting the girl he loves get away, and his hope that her new man gives her the love he didn't give her when they were together. "When I Was Your Man" topped the charts all over the world.

Bruno Mars attended *The Twilight Saga: Breaking Dawn: Part 1* premiere in Los Angeles on November 14, 2011.

Movie Success

Bruno's music has hit the big screen! A number of his songs have been featured in many hit movies and TV shows. In the fall of 2011, a new single entitled "It Will Rain" was released. The song, written and produced by Bruno Mars and The Smeezingtons, appeared on the soundtrack for the film *The Twilight Saga: Breaking Dawn: Part 1*. The music video for the song features scenes from the movie.

23

Saturday Night Live

The first time Bruno performed "Locked Out Of Heaven" live was on *Saturday Night Live* on October 20, 2012. He also sang "Young Girls" from the album. That night he was the host of the show, as well as the musical guest. Critics and fans praised Bruno and his band for their performances. Bruno also proved that he is comfortable acting in front of an audience. His acting was spot-on, and he kept the audience laughing throughout his **skits**.

RIO 2

Listen for Bruno's voice as a character of a bird in the new movie *Rio 2*. This **animated** movie is a **sequel** to the previous 2011 movie *Rio. Rio 2* is scheduled to open in theaters in April 2014.

The Cleveland Show

Bruno also became an animated character in the season premiere of *The Cleveland Show*, which aired October 21, 2012. His voice can be heard alongside other musicians such as will.i.am and Nicki Minaj.

A clip from the season 4 premiere of *The Cleveland Show* features will.i.am (left), QuestLove, Nicki Minaj, and Bruno Mars (right).

Released

On December 6, 2012, *Unorthodox Jukebox* was officially released. Since then, the album has sold over one million copies worldwide. Although some songs on the album are traditional love songs, others deal with dark and **risqué** subjects.

On Tour

Bruno has embarked on his second concert tour called The Moonshine Jungle Tour to promote *Unorthodox Jukebox*. He and his band will be performing 87 shows in total. It began on June 22, 2013, and will conclude in the winter of 2014. Fans in North America, Europe, and **Oceania** will have the chance to experience Bruno's spectacular live show.

While on The Moonshine Jungle Tour, Bruno and his band will be wearing suits created by Italian designers Dolce & Gabbana. The designs were inspired by Bruno's music.

Losing His Mother

On June 1, 2013, Bruno Mars lost an important woman in his life. His mother Bernadette passed away suddenly in Hawaii from a **brain aneurysm**. She was only 55 years old. Bruno's mother has always encouraged his love of music and performing. Bruno even recognized this at just four years of age when he wrote a song called "I Love You, Mom" to thank her for all her love and encouragement.

Someone to Lean On

Bruno was fortunate at that time to have the love and support of his long-time girlfriend, fashion model Jessica Caban. The two have been dating since 2011 and are now rumored to be living together in Bruno's $3 million home. Fortunately, Bruno took Jessica to his hometown in July 2012 for a vacation, and his mother got to meet her.

Jessica Caban has been featured in many commercials and fashion magazines.

He Said It

"So thankful for all the love during the most difficult time in my life. I'll be back on my feet again soon. That's what mom wants. She told me."
—Posted to his fans on Twitter on June 6, 2013

Charity Work

Not only does Bruno Mars perform to promote his music, but he also performs in support of various charities. Along with legendary soul singer Aretha Franklin, Bruno played at The Candie's Foundation's benefit gala, which aims to prevent teen pregnancy. He is also a supporter of Musicians On Call, which is an organization that brings live and recorded music to the bedsides of patients in healthcare facilities. Bruno has worked with the **humanitarian** charity Red Cross, as well as The Rainforest Foundation UK, which was founded by Sting and his wife, and aims to protect the world's rainforests and the **indigenous** peoples who live there.

Bruno performs on stage at the Hilarity for Charity event to raise money and awareness for **Alzheimer's disease**.

Future Plans

Although he put out two wildly successful albums, Bruno says that the world hasn't seen anything yet. He would love to collaborate with other major artists including Rihanna, Lady Gaga, Kanye West, Jay-Z, and Mumford & Sons. Bruno also wants to discover the next big talent, and is looking for an artist who inspires him to create, and who he would have fun creating music with. Bruno lives by this philosophy:

"Someone told me something that stuck with me: 'You have to envision your life, and then go backwards.' I've been living by that motto for a while, so I see where I need to be. Now I'm just backtracking and trying to get back up there."

SUPER BOWL SINGER

Bruno Mars is scheduled to perform at **NFL**'s Super Bowl half-time show on February 2, 2014.

Bruno took home two awards at the MTV Video Music Awards on August 25, 2013.

Timeline

1985: Peter Gene Hernandez is born on October 8 in Honolulu, Hawaii

1988: Begins impersonating Elvis Presley with The Love Notes, his family's band

1992: Lands a cameo role in the movie *Honeymoon in Vegas*

2002: Graduates from high school

2003: Moves to Los Angeles, California

2004: Signs with Motown Records, but is later dropped from the label

2009: Bruno Mars, Philip Lawrence, and Ari Levine form The Smeezingtons

2010: Arrested for drug possession in September

2010: The album *Doo-Wops & Hooligans* is released on October 4

2010: The Bruno Mars Live: Doo-Wops & Hooligans Tour begins

2011: "Just the Way You Are" wins the Grammy Award for Best Male Pop Vocal Performance

2011: Begins dating model Jessica Caban

2011: *The Twilight Saga: Breaking Dawn: Part 1* soundtrack is released, featuring the single "It Will Rain"

2012: Appears on *Saturday Night Live* as musical guest and host

2012: Provides the voice of his character on *The Cleveland Show*

2012: The album *Unorthodox Jukebox* is released on December 6

2013: Bruno's mother Bernadette Hernandez passes away in Hawaii on June 1

2013: The Moonshine Jungle Tour begins

2014: Performs during the halftime show at NFL's Super Bowl XLVIII

2014: Provides the voice for a character in the movie *Rio 2*

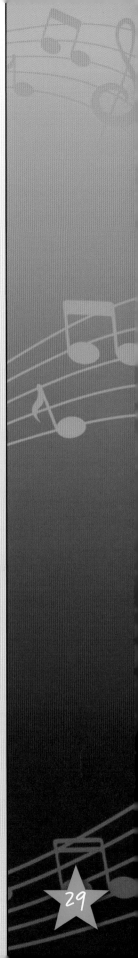

29

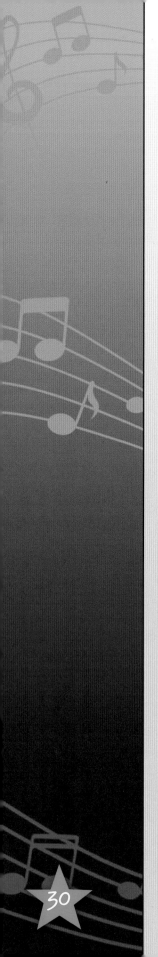

Glossary

Alzheimer's disease The most common form of dementia, or memory loss, for which there is no cure

animated Computer-generated cartoons

artists and repertoire (A&R) manager The person at a record label responsible for finding talent and overseeing the artistic development of the artists

ballad A form of narrative verse set to music, usually of a romantic nature

brain aneurysm A blood vessel in the brain that has dilated with blood due to disease or the weakening of the blood vessel's wall

cameo A brief appearance

disillusioned To be disappointed when proven to be incorrect about a view or assumption

engineer A person who plans and designs engines, roads, bridges, dams, or machines

genres Categories

humanitarian A person or organization devoted to the welfare of human beings

immigrate To move to another country

indigenous Native to an environment

leg The stage of a journey

NFL National Football League

Oceania The islands of the southern, western, and central Pacific Ocean

percussionist The member of a band who plays an instrument that is sounded by being struck or scraped by a beater

producer An individual within the music industry who is responsible for managing the recording of an artist's music

promote To help sell or popularize

risqué Something that suggests impropriety

sequel An artistic work that continues the story of an earlier work

signature A distinctive characteristic

skit A short theatrical sketch

stereotype An oversimplified image of a type or class of person or thing

versatile Able to do many things competently

Find Out More

Books

Higgins, Nadia. *Bruno Mars: Pop Singer and Producer* (Pop Culture Bios). Learner Classroom, 2012.

Leavitt, Aimie, *Bruno Mars* (Blue Banner Biographies), Mitchell Lane Publishers, 2012.

Tieck, Sarah. *Bruno Mars: Popular Singer & Songwriter* (Big Buddy Biographies). ABDO Publishing, 2012.

Websites

Bruno Mars
www.brunomars.com
Bruno Mars's official website

www.myspace.com/brunomars
Bruno Mars's official profile, which includes latest music, albums, music videos, and updates

Twitter
https://twitter.com/BrunoMars
Bruno Mars on Twitter

Index

About the Author

Adrianna holds degrees in English Language and Literature and Fine Arts and has a diploma in Professional Writing. Her professional career includes working as an editor for Crabtree Publishing and authoring many non-fiction books for children. Adrianna is currently a freelance writer and editor, and has completed her first children's fiction chapter book.